THE BONES OF THE EARTH

For My Father
Howard Eugene Berry
(1924–1982)

THE BONES OF THE EARTH
Carol Jane Bangs

A NEW DIRECTIONS BOOK

ACKNOWLEDGMENTS

Grateful acknowledgment is made to the editors and publishers of the following journals in which some of these poems first appeared: *Calyx, Rendezvous,* and *The Stony Thursday Review.*

"Love in the Middle Ages" and "Bathing the Baby" first appeared in *Irreconcilable Differences,* a limited edition chapbook published by Confluence Press in 1978.

The quotations at the beginning of each section are *letras* of flamenco cante recorded by D. E. Pohren in his book *The Art of Flamenco,* copyright © 1967.

Special thanks to Jim Heynen, Kim Stafford, Bob and Linda Clifton, and the rest of the family everywhere.

Manufactured in the United States of America
First published as New Directions Paperbook 563 in 1983
Published simultaneously in Canada by George J. McLeod, Ltd., Toronto

Library of Congress Cataloging in Publication Data
Bangs, Carol Jane, 1949–
    The bones of the Earth.
    "A New Directions book."
    I. Title.
PS3552.A4755B6 1983   811'.54   83–12128
ISBN 0–8112–0883–4 (pbk.)

New Directions Books are published for James Laughlin
by New Directions Publishing Corporation
80 Eighth Avenue, New York 10011

TABLE OF CONTENTS

I

El libro de la experiencia
no sirve al hombre de ná;
al final viene la letra
y nadie llega al final.

Remembrance Day

I was not born when my father came
alone to the Norfolk coast,
drawn back to his ancestors by a war
he only talks about when drinking
or after a funeral.
Here, on a landscape like eastern Nebraska,
he lived three years in metal quonsets
and never swam in the sea.   .

Thirty years later the village church
still promises never to fall.
Green needles of winter wheat
push through crusted brown fields
and smoke from the crematorium
rises past housing estates.
In a corner, near the council allotments,
an old man wheels turnips to a shed.
The roof, under its vines and moss,
is corrugated quonset tin.

And in Norwich this morning the red sun
rises through leafless elms.
My daughter peels a tangerine.
I light a cigarette.
In my father's attic are photographs
of German cities he bombed.
Above the maze of streets and steeples
each hit is a puff of smoke
rising toward the camera.

Downslope

"You see them a lot, up in the Sawtooth,
them elk with upslope legs come in a little
short. It's walkin' around the mountains
does it. That's where them rings come
from—makes the hills look like they're
screwed to the ground."—an Idaho rancher

On every mountain the brown neckchains,
slopes split open in parallels
of clockwise migration.

I, too, walk that drunkline,
balance on what doesn't meet,
headlights, tidelines, moonlit bridges.
I follow the ends of my fingernails,
ten spades lifting the heavy air
like last year's mulch,
ten knives ripping to brown grosgrain
the soft green mountainsides.

When the world rolls over
onto its belly
I ride it like a barrel,
dig in with nail and cleat.
The sound of the head is
a seed-dry gourd,
the voice a rush of unseen water
plunging over glacial cliffs.
The tiny ocean behind the eardrum
shifts to match a new tide
and I lean by degrees
against that hand
stretching lakes to waterfalls,
bear down hard on the upslope leg,
firstborn, closest to earth.
I pay for this unexpected landfall,
not with a sense of renewal,
but with a history of deliberate descent.
Migrating South these impossible fences,
I get a new slant on the territory.
I learn to walk with a limp.

The Meadow

Winter Solstice

Across the meadow silver with frost
a rustle of sticks giving way.
It is not the moon
come stalking,
one hand over its eyes.
It is not the last
star of morning falling
in the litter of briars.

Across the midwinter stubble
a solitary white shadow
obscures the thin willow limbs.
One by one the dark lines submerge;
one by one they reappear,
brushed with thin whips of light.

As if in a dream the white horse
approaches the open field,
bends its head to the taste of salt,
turns and opens its wings.

From the darkness of the earth
I watch it slowly ascend.
On each tiny leaf a white hand
reaches toward its star.

A Few Miles North of Union

I think it was March, or earlier,
but summer was a long way off,
when we pulled over beside the Sound
between Hoodsport and Union.
Hours of talking while the children slept—
our voices were gray as the ebbing tide,
blank as the winter sky.

Just off the beach, oyster strings
dangled in icy rows, their scarecrow
scaffolding propped by booms
of thick fir and Western Cedar,
and the shoreline glimmered
with clastic litter,
fragments of milky shell.
In the shallows we cupped up
tiny floaters, colonies of cells,
zygotes of some unknown species
clouding the pools near our feet.

You found a stone,
skipped it over the ripples,
then turned to show me how,
filling in a childhood emptiness
I'd always taken for granted,
the smooth cold slipping past my fingers,
the easy, loping arc,
the skittery dance from here to there,
the flat water shattered to rings
that cross and recross forever.

At our feet a thousand dumb stones
rotated with the daylight;
our shadows filled each hole and crevice
with their persistent currents,
and our voices murmured in our chests
without coming up for air.
Later, I remembered the feel
of those stones, the shimmering
cold water, and everything
I didn't say because
it was so important to be right.

Genesis

At the Seattle Aquarium, 1981

Cow Fish, they call them, these bright caskets
whose swivel-eyes penetrate the gloom
for weaker, less luminous jewels.
They are their own treasure,
these rotund chunks of topaz
with fierce, improbable horns.
Nothing like cows on the old farm, you say,
and we turn past the series of bubbling windows
where tetras perform electric ballets
and flashlight fish aim their sockets
at the fingers of touring schoolchildren.

The corridor slopes like an ocean beach,
past salt marshes and estuaries.
In the tidepools those troublesome lower forms
spread their vivid, gelatinous bodies
safe from our nervous fingers.
From here we can't see those intricate
egg-spirals aping the works of clocks,
neonate hydras cocooned in aspic,
water-fields sown with white teeth.
Reproduction regains its mystery
under sea-lettuce, eel grass, and mud.

But where the hallway rises to light
we look up to the concrete river,
the holding-tank headwater of the ladder
where salmon nurslings churn the brine
before plunging down the tunnel
for seven years at sea.
Close by the overhanging wall,
two spawners drift in the lull.

The battered female, fat with eggs,
nudges the smooth, cold glass.
The male, his steely sides bulging scarlet,

opens and closes his hooked lower jaw
as if trying to take it off.
Together they measure the perimeter
of their skylit bed,
avoiding the thick water near the center,
where, through masses of trapped air,
the sun thrusts a long white arm.
We take the side door,
exiting slowly
into separate atmospheres.

The Orphanage

You don't remember what path it was
led you past the tumble-down houses
and roadblocks thirty years old,
just that the orphanage still stands,
its sunset bricks rising three stories
from acres of ragged lawn.
You enter through the broken panes,
follow an invisible thread
from room to cell-like room,
the only spelunking a city boy knows,
aiming the torch of your attention
at dusty artifacts, tracing
the scratches in rotting plaster
for some word you recognize.

When you enter you don't know
the room you are looking for,
until you find it, dark-cellared,
gleams of light poised on cracked rims
of a dozen porcelain tubs,
each one sized for a tiny body's
institutional cleanliness.
You see them then, the awkward girls
with lank hair and nothing on their minds,
bathing sick children in dull resentment,
a weekly baptismal despair.
And you say you won't return
to this dark room,
yourself alone,
orphaned by such small deaths
this could be your home.

You want to believe the concrete freeways
looping under and over that ground,
the cold metal twisted against the railing,
the clean detachment of speed,
knowing all along silver poplars
still border that gravel drive,
knowing all along your soul inhabits
at least one other world.
Hands on the wheel, pushing 50,
you hear the stones beneath your feet.
You run as fast as you can.

On Translation 1: Deep Song

The printed slip tumbling from the earphone box
misspells in four languages a warning
either to limit the tape deck volume
or to avoid excesses of the heart,
depending on the translator's bias.
You wonder at this lapse in technology,
a message naive as your childhood crickets
turned belly-up under failed legs for the
post-mortem verdict reserved for tin imports
and the expectations of love.

In the kitchen they are stirring coffee;
the little clicks of spoon on cup
punctuate this foreign music
you want to pour into this woman's blood
as she leans expectantly toward
the machine which carried no apologies.
She hears the elusive girlish giggles,
the primitive recording of lively song,
a barefoot andalucian teenager coaxed
to trill acapella into the microphone,
marking time between the verses
with mimicked rhythmic strums,
echoing that *sevillanas* you just finished
making over again on tight strings,
a morse code of *compas, salida,* and *copla*
pulsed into the night from a well-lit room
in a safe, small American town.
All this music, this encoding
and decoding, translation done over
and over again, as if the pure test
only awaited time and a minimum faith.

At home, your autobiography
revises itself in the mirror,
your son bent over his guitar,
its new wires connected to a device
which repeats each sound too late,
returning each note of that same flamenco
to the history from which it was plucked.
In the glow of a heatlamp pieces of zebrawood

fuse into one; in the cookpot an old axe
swims in black pond water for no reason
except to remind you that some strings
are never really cut; every road walked,
every idea or child fathered
in carelessness, joy, or need,
tumbles in this roiling dark;
everything the hands join together,
everything they articulate,
simmers here in the water, the mirror,
in faces raised to the night sky
where the crescent of Venus rides a crescent moon.
Each note recorded and erased still sounds
through your dreams, your body, these words,
these stirrings making constellations,
these intervals making deep song
from distance utterances.

II

A un sabio le pregunté
y me contestó al momento
"yo también me enamoré
y aunque me sobra el talento
lloro por una mujer."

Invitation

In darkness I reach out to you
with the deliberate satisfaction of a needle
slipped through tight-woven cloth,
the misleading ease of a bean seed
raising its cotyledon flag,
the patience of the caterpiller
rolled up in its gauzy muff,
the upstream tenacity of the salmon
climbing rainbows across steep falls,
with the heart-beat and hand-clasp
of the best of us humans,
masculine, feminine, riding the line,
everything reaching past borders and fencelines,
coagulants, alloys, infusions,
the blood-lines traced in black and white palms,
the seed lines traced in young and old faces,
the life-line, heart-line, head-line predictors
of the best and worst to come,
with the faithlessness of a drop of water
tumbling off a curled spring leaf,
the faith of a hundred drops of water
roaring through caverns of stone,
with the sun and stars punching holes in darkness
like needles, or outstretched hands.

Love After Anger

Lying beside you I hear the wind
combing the trees of distant mountains
far from these arid arguments
in which we wander, love's nomads,
pitching and breaking our frail camps
on the contours of mood and intent.

I smell that green lake where salamanders
break the surface to silver fans
with their prehensile twist and dip.
We are not so distant in our sliding
across the faces of our needs,
searching for those lulls when,
through a silence deeper than sleep,
all we are windows itself at once
and we see with the body's lucid eyes
past personality's mutable weather.

Your lips comb the forests of my thighs.
Between sloped walls of flesh your breath
clouds over us like mountain steam.
For you, now, I would disown those diamonds
imbedded in the dark coal of common sense,
would give you my belly like a meadow,
call you like a deer to browse.

I give my body to the compass of your hands,
reveal in a voice cracked as the raven's
that wilderness under my skin,
blood rivers coursing their red canyons,
arroyos and dusky plateaus.
You are the stone, the rod, and the serpent.
I am that river springing out of a stone,
irrigating these deserts of night,
scattering armfuls of roses.

Ritual for an Absent Lover

for James

The sun comes up a half-hour early.
Leaning from the window I think of you,
wondering if, where you rest your head,
the sun sets your hair on fire.

Love is light, whose first intimations
startle the dreaming houses and trees,
moving with sure, predictable measure
toward the darkness where all begins.

Whatever light the body turns to,
climbing up from its lonely sleep,
leads us toward nothing but itself,
the cold generations of space.

Before your eyes lift from their bed
of whatever pleasure or pain,
turn to that shadow lying warm beside you,
that hollow where your body begins.

Let your breath linger in your hair.
Run your hand over your belly.
Teach your skin language it will remember
in the babel of anonymous crowds.

When you rise to your window, do not think of me;
bolt the sash and draw the blinds.
When we meet in the distant treaties of night
our bodies will make their own light.

Poem Without the Word "Heart"

There is no other word so useful,
a semantic expansion file mouthing out
all those sensations relevant as bread,
important enough to puzzle us,
though their energy is profligate as yeast.

How often I have looked at your hands
without saying how remarkable they are.
How often your mouth has covered mine
so tightly I forget our breathing
is no more than subtle translation,
a language fat with verbs and adverbs
defined only in reference to themselves.
How often I have felt your body
stretching the limits of my skin
though you swam or danced or ran
beyond the science of touch.

Were I to survey the catalogue,
the ABCderium of love,
each nerve would speak its memorized piece,
then withdraw to its corner of the stage;
cell after cell would multiply in silence,
never knowing it made a difference.

It is what our dozen voices
say to themselves in private,
the distance our bodies cannot reach
no matter how hard they try,
this tongue fumbling against the ribs,
this bowl emptied as fast as it fills,
this verb we bend into a noun,
the word this poem does not include
because it is everywhere else.

Leaving You by Water

This is the motion I would teach you,
this slow shuffle over water wiped
smooth as a pewter plate, the full tide
thrusting a lifetime of weather
toward the bright arms of morning sun.

Above the bow a mottled gull
divides the wind with level wings
and a short, sour cry.
The current he travels is constant departure;
he turns as the rope hits the pier.

The tide, too, knows no home
but the path of a gypsy moon.
Soon it will ebb toward your shore,
the soft blur of fir on the headland.
When it does you will be there to meet it,
walking the gravel and oystershell beach.
You will watch for a hour the unconscious jellyfish
ballooning ahead like a pair of lungs,
learning that motion in parts of your body
you never connected with love.
For the first time you will understand.
You will watch the tide climb the black pilings
and you will have no regrets.

At Discovery Bay in April

for R. M. C.

I might as well be a fiddlehead,
a scouring rush poking thick fingers
to test the softening air,
moist tendrils swaying,
tongues shooting forth,
a willow letting down its ragged hem,
for the green world rises to song
on this, a day in early April,
filled with every living fluid,
alive with the random agitation
of that swarm of midges
clustered low near the pond,
their bodies mingled in abstract dance
choreographed by melting ice.

Nor are they subtle, these arrogant firs,
a fleet of masts rising into the gray
that could be sky or water, so vague
are its origins, so humid its touch.
Like the priest hanging flags
of the cross and the fishes,
I bless each living thing setting forth
on a journey into new seasons,
knowing all will distill in that final harvest
when each fisher empties his deepest hold
and the grain lies heaped in a broad meadow
glowing hot under autumn sun.

What then will be our accounting;
will we blame these woods, this season,
our hands moving into each other
like eyeless amphibians,
blind to all but waking heat,
or will we reach into that water
where drowned trees slumber down centuries,
their life stories circled in stone?
They stretch like cables,

linking these mirrors, water and sky,
where we circle on redoubled surfaces,
seeing in each other's widening eyes
the steadily lengthening shadows.

Touching Each Other's Surfaces

Skin meeting skin, we want to think
we know each other scientifically;
we want to believe
it is objective knowledge
gives this conviction of intimacy,
makes us say it feels so right.
That mole below your shoulder blade,
the soft hair over my thighs—
we examine our bodies with the precision
known only to lovers or surgeons,
all those whose profession is explication,
who have to believe their own words.
And yet, having memorized each turning,
each place where bone strains or bends,
each hollow, each hair, each failure of form,
we still encounter that stubborn wall,
that barrier which hides an infinite vastness
the most sincere gesture can't find.

Nor does emotion take us further
than the shared heat of bodies
aware of themselves,
the flattery of multiple desires.
We rest in each other's arms unexplained
by these currents of feeling rushing past
like ripples over a pool of water
whose substance never changes,
reflecting each wave, each ribboned crossing,
without being really moved.
We search each other's eyes so long

beyond our own reflections,
finding only the black centers,
the immeasurable interior we'll
never reach with candle,
never plumb with love.

Perhaps it is just this ignorance,
this absence of certainty, lack of clear view,
more than anything, brings us together,
draws us into and through each other
to the unknown inside us all,
that gray space from which
what we know of ourselves
emerges briefly, casts a transient
shadow across the earth
and learns to believe in itself just enough
to believe in some one else.

Love in the Middle Ages

This hand I give you is an allegory.
In the Middle Ages
love had three meanings
and any one would do.
Dante fell in love
with a prepubescent who
showed him paradise.
Not everyone in the Middle Ages
was a poet or a saint.
I say it's worth it,
kneeling down,
if you've something to look up to.
You say it wasn't easy—
stiff knees, wet floors,
a cold ache between the sheets.
For one thing they knew that sex
isn't everything, that love
was the first word God memorized.
This hand I give you is an allegory.
Let me teach it to you.

III

Entré un día en un manicomio
me pesa el haberlo hecho
yo ví una loca en el patio
se sacaba y daba el pecho
a una muñequita de trapo . . .

Virginity

No one tells you the real hymen
sometimes stretches so thin
you hardly know it's there
except for this pain, filling your body
when you think you are not loved.
When the lumps swell your breasts like
clusters of grapes and you flinch
at your lover's touch, who will tell you
it is not milk your body is weeping
though you feel it, tidal, leading your heart
as if to a child's stubborn cry.

Violence is never beautiful,
not the wound rising under the skin
like ink blossoming over a blotter,
not the dull nag of muscle on bone.
You think you'll never dance again
to that drumbeat lifting you past time
into the corridors of night
where maidens swing voluminous skirts,
ingenuous, wholly virgin.

In the house you move from room to room,
taking inventory of books and flowers,
counting cups, spoons, and gloves,
knowing you live in none of these,
not even the garden which breathes with you,
the poppies nodding with drowsy milk,
the roses entwining the yew.
The act of looking is barbed wire.
You can't break past though your hands
open their flesh like plums.
To be a woman in possession of herself—
against whom is that crime committed?

When you place your hand
on your breast the pain
makes you wonder who has died
and how you could have forgotten.
Your mouth vowels out its love

though no one is near.
There, in that gesture, you find yourself,
find a reason for the pain, knowing
you could never face again
that stillbirth of the emotions,
sorrow we don't understand.

Not like our men, dowsing love's labyrinths
for that narrow stream back to their mothers,
we women catalogue our losses, seeking
in each new explosion of space
the shadow of what cannot be given,
that pearl without price Mother spoke of,
thinking she meant something else.
When you find it, wrapped in seaweed
at the bottom of a dream, all the fences
will disappear, though you will not notice,
having no need to be anywhere
other than where you are.

Poem for a Woman of Forty

What can I tell you of this journey
but that it is half over
before you know you've begun.
Woman, your breasts are dull spears,
poor protection against that light
circling every inch of your body,
probing even the secret cells
where mismatched chromosomes
spar and rub to
the lunar music of blood.

While you sit bent in your flowered chair,
waiting for lovers to call,
your industrious body is making itself,
creating muscles, organs, bones,
and that dark, pear-shaped room
where the turbines spin and slow again
in intermittent red flood.

Silence turns your ear to the body's music,
the sound your knees make, coming together,
the sound as they move apart.
The journey does not have to begin.
We walk as we have always walked;
suddenly we notice our feet
and where our feet are aimed.

Woman, while I am talking to you
whole colonies of cells are dying,
borne by dark streams to the kidneys,
filtered toward the light.
From left or right ovary another seed
drops into those eager fingers,
begins the long slope into life
or the tumble to zero.

The pain of each step is forgotten
before the other foot drops.
Time measures flesh like a long-lost sister

whose fingers leave delicate marks.
Each word divides itself, multiplies
in the brain's deep cavern
where light excavates no more truth
than a full moon cast back by the sea.
Only at the end does this path become clear,
the short and long of a single highway,
the ever-after of birth.

Woman Taking Down Laundry

This is the portrait
Brueghel never painted,
this woman with long arms;
she could gather the sky.

The cloud-colored apron
embraces her belly
as she rises on her toes.
Her tweed skirt slowly lifts
to bare her rumpled knees
as she sidesteps down the hallway
between great sails of sheets,
humming beneath her breath
a song of harvest and praise.

It is the rhythm
of a rocking cradle;
hands reach out,
loosen the pins,
bundle the fabric to her breast
like a baby, a loaf of bread.
One by one the socks are mated,
hems come together.

Clouds gather on the horizon,
a gray and white armada.
The wind reaches

under her skirt.
The basket fills.
When she turns toward the house
her dark breasts
float on a mountain of snow.
Her hair rises in black wings
and the wide saucer of her face
lifts to catch the first rain.

Bathing the Baby

I lift my daughter into the tub,
the element we drew her from
like a fish drawn into a net,
her blue-veined head
streaked with my blood,
the dark cord gently uncoiled,
remembering the fear in your throat
as her purple lips first tasted air.

Did you think of the drowning child
your mouth could not revive,
the dead baby you thumped and rubbed
as the legs stiffened in your hands?
Did you think of the incoherent mother,
the curds of soap stuck to the feet?
Was it the memory of death by water
that made you carry your own child
to the wide lap of the Pacific?
You sprinkled brine on her forehead;
the tide rose blue in her eyes,
and we saw in that face the island
where two oceans swam together,
something already stronger than fear,

a pearl tumbling from its white-lipped shell,
already too deep to retrieve.

Each day we repeat this ritual,
and as I sprinkle clear water
over her smooth warm flesh,
she bends her mouth
to kiss the water
and her thin ribs
pulse like gills
under my careful hands.

Middle Child

The woman who swung
the silver needle
over my swelling belly
predicted daughter, son, daughter,
the first already born.
Two weeks later
you lie in this dish,
so small your ambiguous sex
can't prove her right or wrong.
You've come loose from my body
like a finger, the nerves
gone numb and cold.

Your bulging blood-pump,
undersized jaw,
nubs of legs, arms, hands,
batted like fins, naked paws
against that squeeze,
that merciless fist,
that plunge into light.
Little homunculus,
bloody poppet,
tangled in your scarlet ribbons

you're a cuttlefish
netted in red kelp,
beached up at midnight tide.

Is this world so different
from that silver pool
your short legs troubled
with bicycling poise?
Too small to reach my belly's edge,
I never felt you quicken,
but your dreams spilled
into mine, sweet wine
too rare for the cup.

Next month, when the moon
puts its mouth to my veins,
I'll shed my thin velvet coat.
Kneeling by the sea
I'll stitch a blanket
to cover the doorway you've left,
my yarn a hank of black sea grass,
my needle an old woman's wail.

Sleeping with My Children

When I come to bed, Emily is there,
rolled up in the down wrap she calls a "comfy,"
hugging her Peter Rabbit and Volume A
of an encyclopedia, the one with the color
transparencies of the human body.
Earlier she had asked about the heart,
why it has four parts. Now she slumbers
in the light of a small bulb filtered
through a chambered nautilus shell.
I do not move her as I usually would,
back to her own high-legged bed,
but keep her near me, her warm breath
moving the hairs on my neck as I, too,
drift into other worlds. Somewhere
in the night we join again, in one
of those worlds, and she stirs, as I stir,
and we both wake to see the stars lift
for one moment out of the mist, then
submerge, as we submerge, into morning sleep.
When we wake, Geoffrey has joined us,
as well as the two cats. For a moment,
in half light, it seems a cavern too far
back for history, these humans coiled
into their dreams, wary-eyed felines
giving up just enough to share mammal heat.
I love these children as if my heart
would burst, not from sentiment, but from
compassion, the knowledge of their lives
stretching out and away where I cannot
hold them or keep away wounds and fears.
Yet, in the darkness, I give them my faith.
Suckling them I felt my blood turn to milk;
I felt my own death hovering, giving birth
to such mortal flesh. I want to say,
Emily, the heart has four parts
because we haven't room for more.

Neahkahnie, '82

A six-part journal

1

Cancer, she says, here.
Placing her hands
under her breasts,
lifting them like goblets.
No one told me
the body, too,
gets out of bounds like
children or lovers
who don't understand.
One day the small cells shift
in their honeycombs of salt,
lean toward the light
like sun-starved leaves,
thickening like thumbs.
No word to hold them back
once the tide has tasted land,
the wind stuck its
nose in the hedge.
The beach is littered
with translucent cadavers
that once lived,
as we do now,
by subtle adjustment
and jellyfish nerve.
These dimples are not
from smiling, she says,
smoothing the rumpled
pillows of skin.
When the goblets are gone
where will we pour the wine?
Not listening now
for any answer, turning
her head toward the chugging sea,
neck veins pulsing blue
as the incoming tide.
From the bag I have brought
I lift ripe peaches,
placing them one by one
on the deep green plate.

"I didn't believe it
until I heard the name."
Only with words do we feel
the extravagance of pain;
the word "saffron"
rides on the tongue,
a rich biscuit,
bumblebees gilded
with drowsy pollen.
"Crocus" is an opening,
light, a fist unclenching,
pale fingers reaching
toward a dangling peach,
September wakings,
the sun daybreak red.
We teach our children
the proper vowels,
opening wounds of
frustrated love
no alphabet will salve.
Looking up they say
"cloud," "weather,"
where before they drifted
under the surface,
reflections of themselves.
One by one the mouth attempts
anger, pity, devotion,
emotions accreting like
oystershell, nacre,
mother-of-pearl spit
out between the teeth:
"I want no dish that is broken."

3

"I never liked mirrors,"
she says, standing naked,
"all this too much on one side."
As she touches eyelid,
nipple, thigh, she
names them as a mother
teaches an infant,
placing the body in the air
one piece at a time.
"One should know oneself
from the inside out,
not the other way.
When I first made love
to a man I saw
my breasts in his hands
like dough, kneaded
and worked that way,
and they didn't seem
to be mine anymore.
When the baby sucked
his mouth pulled so tight
I thought he'd draw
my whole body in
one piece at a time,
but then he'd let go,
all at once, his mouth
corners drooling milk;
the nipples would snap back
into the flesh, elastic,
blue as plums.
Sometimes I wanted to
take them off, overfull,
blue-veined udders.
Empty, they hung on my chest
like the waterbags old cars
slung over their fenders
crossing the Mojave."
Now she lifts them tenderly.
"They never seemed mine before."

4

A woman gave birth to a woman
who gave birth to me,
my nipples small and tight
on the jungle-gym of ribs,
mother's breasts filling her shirt
as she sweated the coastal incline,
grandmother strapping herself in gauze
to fit a flapper's gown,
until her breasts retreated
leaving only the mark of their tide.
It was before they clearcut
Tillamook Head, that mountain
eaten by white-toothed seas,
before the old-growth
cedar fell screaming
its awful bark-rip curse,
that embarrassed moment
when the headland
exhaled in grunting sighs.
The moss was so thick
our hands lost themselves
in the vagueness of rocks and logs.
We walked as if on pliant bodies
whose breath rose between our legs,
warm and humid and near.
Two mothers, two daughters,
the three of us hand
over hand up basalt,
easing down green deer slides,
through tunnels of time and age,
ambiguities of weather.
Three women turned inside out
in subtle, persistent motion,
crossing the mountain
between morning and evening,
from north to south.
At Ecola we emerged together
in sunlight, lizard-hot
bodies on angled cliff stone,
taking off our shirts to dry,

drinking from lichen-lipped falls.
From the bag I took peaches,
ripe and warm, pulling
the flesh into dripping chunks,
letting the thick juice run.

5
Talking to a woman, like eating,
sustains us in spite of our guilt,
as if the daylight gestures betray
dark messages, hunger and need.
There is a social anorexia
among these women, stripped clean
by life's expected betrayals,
biting their tongues in neat cafes
as if the taste of truth would catch,
lure them into indulgences
of affection and recognition,
fatten them past the reach of men
into each other's arms.
Out the window I watch ripe pears
drop from her well-tended trees.
In everything she does not say
I hear my own confessions.

To the young nurse she babbles
of labor pains, green curtains
and the brilliant tropical fish
glimpsed in those demerol seas.
Always before she left the white walls
with more than she could hold,
the warm bundle on her breast,
the bags and baskets of fruit.
Is it really that she is diminished
or that these awkward visitors,
looking anywhere but at her body
newly smoothed into sheets,
have lost parts of themselves
calipers can't measure?
Her tongue is not bruised.
When she lifts her voice
from the avenues of sleep
it rings out like taxi horns,
shrill, demanding notice.
To her side she calls us,
friends, sisters, children,
holds us to her chest
until she cries with the pain
and we cry too, discovering
the same stubborn thrust of heart,
the same ecstacy of breath.

The Wicked Witch

. . . to the wise
Often, often is it denied
To be beautiful or good.
                    —W. H. Auden, "Oxford"

She greets her mirror, eager as a child;
Eighty years pull back to the bone,
the skin drawn thin as paper
over cheek and skull.
Lips part over yellow teeth
ground half down to the gum.
Nostrils open on a black vault.
Thin hair frizzles from her scarf
like a halo of white frost.

And the eyes peer over ravaged lids
like the eyes of a newborn child,
who, having seen all that is,
has everything to forget.
Age draws her closer to the awareness
that the appearance of goodness
is all that we know of the Good.
What use has an old woman for propriety,
her body having failed to give her pleasure,
beauty neither a thing of the past
nor a trusted potential.
She sees in the mirror no more, no less
than what has lived there forever.

History treats her badly, this crone.
She never had victims; they had themselves,
falling under the spell of their own beauty,
stumbling through their own dark forests,
unprepared, no lamp in hand.
The poison apple dropped
from Snow White's own tree.
Hansel's cage grew out of his bones.
Rapunzel's tower was coiled from her plaits

and the Frog Prince fathered no heirs.
Who's to tell what Sleeping Beauty dreamed
before waking to marriage and decorum,
the ennui of ever-after?

These crooked hands could be murderers.
The thin lips could move to deceive.
Lacking goodness or beauty the old woman
knows the roots of the oldest tales.
For a witch knows the world the way it is,
looks into the mirror long past the age
when a princess would look away.

IV

Ay pobre corazón mío . . .
por más gorpes que le doy
nunca se da por vensío . . .

Starting from the Dark

It is not the moon,
nor sun, nor stars,
nor the sound of a voice
flaring like crocus
in the cave of the heart.
Something we've forgotten
rings out like a wedding,
stirring the dim woods and fields.
The sound of bells, coming and going
across the dark water
is suddenly as loud as Easter.

Even with only one eye,
light has a trapper's direction;
one finger pointing, pointing,
needles through the ribs.
Hands freeze on yardsticks of light.
Mouths stall like bread.
No apology loosens that landscape,
our hands a gesture apart.

We come back to the windows of childhood,
those vague squares in attics and closets,
but this time we carry ourselves in cradles
tied with the thick knots of dream.
Once our small hands gathered daylight,
built lighthouses and well-lit roads.
Tonight we lie together in darkness
and don't know where to start.

Sometimes, Talking

for John Liddy

. . . It is
like himself, only visible.

Sometimes, talking with a stranger,
you hear the words
through the bones of your head
as if through miles of underground tunnels
rivers have eaten through stone.
From as far as the back of the earth
where today's shadow sweeps a path
before the punctual sun,
your voice echoes from the faces
of all those awkwardly loved.
Those words uttered in lonely sincerity
rebound with the heaviness of the earth,
the muffled vowels of the dreamer
lost in the pillow's dark caves.

Sometimes, talking with a stranger,
you want to reach out to your voice
while it dangles there between you
lit up with new meaning
as by a photographer's flash.
You want to pluck it from the air,
return it to the warm hollows of the mouth,
extending instead an open palm,
a letter, a loaf of bread,
some object whose shape in any mirror
a stranger could safely believe.

The Order of the Black Chrysanthemum

for Tree

There was no taking of solemn vows
that day you burned your dresses and coats,
climbed naked into the well of your dreams
so silently the wind never slowed
as you passed into that other country
we cannot learn through our skin.

Among the icons of darkness and change
even fixed stars tumble and shift.
You see your face in the face of the sea,
ringed with diamonds of light
that filter through the fingers' sieve
as a melody, overheard,
moves down a darkened street,
scattering silences where it has passed.

No diamonds ring the poise of your neck.
No gold dusts the palms of your hands.
You bend to your work with half-closed eyes,
penciling in each after-image
still throbbing on the retina.
The secrets assumed by friends and lovers
are not so obscure as they seem:
your hair unfurling like a flag,
the tiny weight of your shoes.
On each tightened wrist a blot of ink
feathers out like a hybrid flower.

Grief

It fills the air at evening,
drifts through dark hours into daylight;
we wake from dreams of happiness
into the early white air,
a landscape like a city
carved in silence and stone.
We fall into the arms of strangers
without speaking a word.

It falls gently in those hours
when our guilt at living
brings on tears
that fall on the eyes of the dead,
all those who are not sleeping
but lie stretched on white tables
with foreheads smooth as new snow.
We fall into the arms of strangers
who never speak a word.

Like a river frozen to its bed,
grief stands still at the surface,
but the dark waters underneath
are loud with furious motion,
a downward rushing mass of coldness
in which limbs grow bright, then fail.
Lovers stumble home through white streets,
toward the door at the top of the stairs,
toward the lock that is frozen open,
where they turn to each other
and cry out in different languages.

The Poet Studies Physics

for Guy Murchie

As the milk bursts its electric skin,
spills over the rim and streams
to the floor in a series of varying
pear shapes and globes only a fast
camera sees, or at that peak in trajectory
when the hurled glass seems to pause,
burning our retinas with its existence
before it ceases to exist,
we think we have found it, apparent
luminosity, the wholly logical *now*,
that state Greek logicians worried like meat,
fumbling for some medial bone.

Between the beginning, the first step,
and infinite, breathing worlds,
these things gather together:

a number small as the average family;

the eye of a mountain quail;

a scale that will never balance,
its needle drifting endlessly
to nearer and farther extremes;

the center of the universe;

a boy's pocket, filled with stones;

our pencils attempting these ellipses
with elusive focal points—
coral polyp,
quazar,
treble clef,
rose.

On the Escape of a Crow from a Frozen Snowbank

The Beluga whale turns his abstract belly
toward a sun divorced from sundials.
The wolf on his northern marathon
sweeps past snow-covered pipelines,
stopping at each black-lettered milepost
to lift a casual leg.
An old dog sniffs the doorway,
rubs his nose on the mat and retreats,
finding there some human insult
not to be researched.

Whatever roadmap the body follows,
blooming toward each new death,
can't be bought at any newsstand
in reach of the human heart.

The proud crow finally breaks the crust,
beak-first, wing-tips fluttering;
from the earth he jerks into frozen air,
jet feathers blooming from ice.
While above, the brilliant, lazy stars
adjust themselves by fractions,
exploding in furious white suicides
we'll see in a thousand years.

Harvest

Entering the garden after first frost
they bury the broken vines and stalks,
gather the hard-skinned winter squashes,
the last, black-spotted marrows,
turn the soil back into itself
to relearn the lessons of birth.
The baskets grow heavy on their arms
before they reach the barn.
The body tires of its customary uses
and a man and a woman pause
to watch the sun settle into the hills,
to watch the big moon swell.

As a man and a woman come together
on cold April nights,
stretching their naked bodies
across the fresh-turned furrows
silvered by a growing moon,
so a man and a woman reach out
in a season of unpronounceable bounty,
move into each other and out again,
into the silence of lost gesture,
that language whose translations
never fully satisfy.

Their hands do not touch.
From different angles they watch the moon
as if reading a difficult novel,
seeing at last that the gathering in
distills in the solitary,
the lonely duet with the earth
each body dances toward death,
the hidden music to which Zola's peasants
danced their harvest dance,
the threshing floor trodden by heavy boots,
children puking under the table
from too much new beer,
wives with their breasts
dangling out of their dresses

above the mouths of sleeping infants,
young girls with bloodied thighs
snoring behind mounds of straw,
and the scrape of heavy, rustic fiddles
sawing at the light
from a huge, distant moon.

Sunday Afternoon

I am sitting in the black chair.
For three hours I have not stirred
more than the smallest shefflera leaf
fixing its aim on the window.

I have been reading the poems
of an old, persecuted woman
whose words were ripe Russian pears.
Translation dries them to rich leather,
fragments of skin, tiny seeds.

Whirring machines trouble the air
and I believe what a friend once said—
that silence makes life stand still,
or was it darkness, that last authority,
holding our unspoken grief
under his heavy shirt?

This morning, walking along the tide,
I couldn't stop humming that song,
the chorus that rises
and falls like breathing.
Even if the world should stop,
the checkered circles on the meters
stand still in their glass helmets,
still I would hear her voice,
that sad, unalterable music,
the heavy thumping of this clock
winding down in my pocket.

After a Photograph of Virginia Woolf

Mrs. Ramsey, seated at the window,
did not notice the painter Lily Briscoe
who saw her as line, color, an integral part
of the composition: Window frame, wisteria,
bright glaze of sunlight on ribbons of hair.
She attended instead that stream of photons
uttered by a predictable lighthouse,
taking her pulse to its steady breathing,
its interminable one, two, three.

You, too, wait at a window
like the lens of a telescope
focussed on distant stars.
Those beacons with their squinting glint,
photons limping the last few inches
of a journey eons long,
reflect in your eyes, the pond's dark mirror,
the water condensing on frond and twig.

Each minuscule chip of light,
survivor of near space's murky chaos,
each arrow piercing the bright ozone,
breaking earth's hydrogen necklace,
each light-pulse missing by half a beat
drifting clouds, satellites, fir limbs,
ends its chancy, headlong tumble
in that black cave beneath the cornea,
a sudden shout to the brain.

All this time, a million others,
random fragments of raw energy,
bombard the contours of your face,
creating such texture, light and shadow,
no artist would miss the composition,
were your window facing a slanted easel,
were you watched by sharp blue eyes.

Improvisation at the Town

Midnight, your voice descends
in clatter of beer taps and pool.
An admiring drunk fumbles each
of your fingers for that magic
calloused digits discover.
I search your eyes for another
music you can't predict—
sudden leaps from darkness,
currents vibrant as air struck
by a chorus of plucked strings,
movements needing no agile master
to choreograph their themes.

Do we speak of art or friendship?
Do we have a choice?
We know this meeting's no accident,
any more than the last ferry
clapping the sides of the dock
slid into port without star or compass
through confusion of wind and sea.
We still rehearse an unwritten rhythm
vibrating flesh, bone and skin,
changes we reach for without reflection
in the fastest passages.

Finding your chords on the polished bar
you beckon another draft, meeting
behind the bottles your eyes,
detached as any stranger's.
Slowly we learn the limits of the score.
Our art can only be to become
more and more of what we are.

The Winter Flower

Walking by the river I find a flower
whose name I do not know,
five-petalled, square-stemmed, over-wintering,
first flower of a not-yet-arrived season,
last flower of the old year,
blooming from the depths of a rotted stump
where my grandfather's seven-foot saw
felled the fir in its first growing.

The river was closer in those days,
a young stream by geologic measure,
less than a thousand years old,
still aiming straight for that ocean
a hundred miles away.
The ancestors of this early white flower
scattered their seeds all down the valley,
passed through the bodies of migrating waterfowl,
clung to the fur of traveling beasts.
The seeds of this flower were alive somewhere
as I was a seed in the seed of my mother
the day my grandmother felt her stir
in the white petals of her belly.

All the seeds of all the flowers,
the smallest germ cells, chromosomes,
each separate species recreating itself
in the deep earth of passing time,
each seed living its own story—
wherever we reach they cling to our hands;
wherever we fall our bodies will feed them;
wherever we migrate they will follow,
under the bank where the deep waters flow,
at the center of the desert of nameless flowers,
above the bundled pages of history
tied neatly to the bones of our earth,
below the vast screen of the continuous,
where each star shouts a different name
down those dark alleys at whose ends
human observers crouch behind lenses
like an army waiting for dawn.

The Bones of the Earth

Your hand branches into mine
and I draw it to earth.
Do you feel it, this history
we lie on like a bed?
Our bones meet grass.
The fabric of our flesh
draws from roots and bathes
our quieted veins.
When you say the landscape has no bones
I remember that day in the Tate
where I saw what Turner
was really painting
and my knees gave way.

Landscape without skeleton,
what girders of the heart
hold your leaves and clouds?
What vista of gold and red
swirls across that small canvas
where our eyes shed
their windows of light?
When the moon lifts up its broken face
my skin draws up like a purse
and I slide from your exploring hands
until they catch, knuckle-deep in loam.
The moon's eye sees clean through,
pierces our flat bodies, the grass,
deeper than grass the stone sea,
the dark vault of the Pleistocene
with its full memory of bodies
who once loved on wet grass.
In the graphs of geologic strata
our layer is thinner than ink.

These are the bones of the earth,
a landscape of faces
loosed from their bodies,
shuffled together like dinner plates

or coins of a lost currency.
Their stone impressions worn thin as mica,
microscopic platelets stacked up, end on end,
they reach through rock, through us,
toward the dry, dispassionate moon.

La Vida Verdadera

for Paco

The day the furniture threatens your life
and your house grows down around you,
you fasten on the fact of death,
the human condition in *Hamlet* and *Lear*,
the childhood succession of pets.
You see your children as inheritors
of all you have or are,
just as your mother's large veins
stand up on your clenched hands
and you raise them over your head to drain
in a gesture that frequents your dreams.

You reject the notion that poetry
is more than temporary,
that the intimation of mortality
was cured with a modern vaccine.
Death, that blind mugger
holds the mortgage
on every busstop in town.
Every road leads past a hanging tree
or ends in avalanche.

What you want is a bridge to that life
where daughter, mother, sister fail
as vessels for the absolute,

our knowledge that ripeness always overflows;
the lines we draw no longer make houses,
or roads, or borderlines.

The real life inhabits a territory
with no test for citizenship,
a garden hidden inside a forest
with sundial and summerhouse,
a hillside overlooking the sea,
white with yarrow and spray.
Telling time by sap-clock, sun-clock,
clinging to what opens before us,
we grow upward in spite of ourselves,
a tangle of thin, perennial vines,
blooming on last year's green wood.

IV

Ay pobre corazón mío . . .
por más gorpes que le doy
nunca se da por vensío . . .